Hi. I'm Rosa.

Hi. I'm Taneesha.

Today is Career Day at our school. On Career Day, adults visit our school and talk about their jobs. There is one adult in each classroom. We are going to ask them questions about their jobs. We can go to as many classrooms as we can in one day.

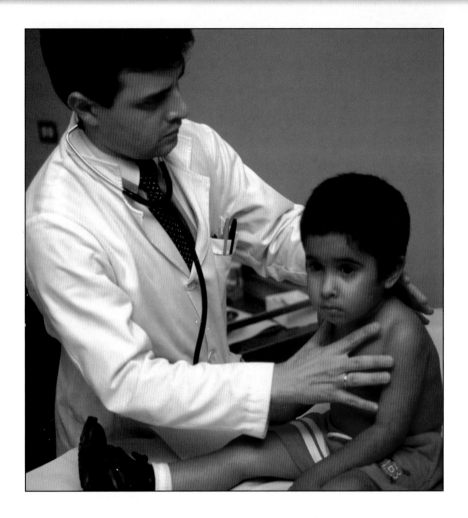

First, we go to Room 111. Dr. Alessandro Simpson is there. He works at Children's Hospital in the pediatrics department. He has worked there for 7 years. He takes care of sick children and helps them get well.

We ask him how long it takes to become a doctor. He tells us doctors go to school for eight years after high school. Then, they study and work in a hospital for two more years.

Next, we go to Room 106. Maria Ramirez is there. She works at a restaurant called Maria's. Ms. Ramirez is a chef.

Ms. Ramirez tells us about her job. She has been a chef since 1999. Chefs prepare food. They choose the menu and cook special dishes. Some chefs go to cooking school. Many chefs learn by doing. They learn "on the job."

Then we go to Room 117. Tyrone Jones is a firefighter. Firefighters put out fires and rescue people from burning buildings. They often rescue people in car accidents.

Mr. Jones shows us some of his equipment and some pictures of firefighters. He tells us firefighters have to be strong. Hoses often weigh more than 100 pounds.

We ask him why he is a firefighter. He tells us he wants to keep people safe, and he wants to help them if they are in danger. Firefighters are very helpful.

After that, we visit Karen Smith in Room 212. Ms. Smith is a carpenter. She repairs old buildings. She takes down and rebuilds old walls. She builds new kitchens or bathrooms in old houses or apartment buildings. She has worked on many beautiful houses.

She shows us some of her tools. She has hammers, nails, wrenches, and safety goggles. In this picture, she is using a chain saw. She tells us she likes to make things. She likes to help people fix their houses.

Then, we go to Room 220. Stan Johnson is there. He's an artist. He draws and paints pictures of birds, animals, and landscapes. Many people have bought his paintings.

We ask Mr. Johnson how we can become artists. He tells us that artists should first learn to draw and then learn to paint. Artists should always carry a pencil and notebook with them. When they see something interesting, they can draw it. Mr. Johnson tells us to draw something every day.

Finally, we return to our homeroom. Our teacher is there. She is writing our homework on the board.

We ask Mrs. Chen why she is a teacher. She tells us she likes watching students learn.

Mrs. Chen gives us our homework. We should write a paper about Career Day. We should write about the different careers and hand in our papers on Friday.

Questions

A. Do you understand? Write your answers on a piece of paper.

1. Where does Dr. Simpson work?

2. What do chefs do?

3. Who is a carpenter?

4. What does Stan Johnson paint?

B. Word Study

1. These words are object pronouns. Find these object pronouns in the story.

   him   her   it   us   them

2. Find words that use the suffixes **er, or, ist.**

   teacher

C. Check Your Work

Compare your answers with your teacher's answers. Correct your mistakes.